Foreword

PROOF ALL THINGS DO WORK TOGETHER TO THEM WHO BELIEVE

Take God's Plan Out of the Can is an incredible read. This book will inspire you to try again. It is the enemy's job to stop and block what God has in store for you. However, Author *Tameka Bullock* is living proof that no matter the challenges or obstacles, with God all things are possible. I am very proud of the way she has chosen to not be a victim. Her book will tell of her triumphs and victories over what the devil thought would wipe her out. Dear reader, it's time for you to go back to what you started because through this book you will learn that if you do you will win.

-Apostle Julia D. Ford, Assistant Pastor of
True Love Church

TAMEKA R. BULLOCK

Plan
TAKE GOD'S
OUT OF THE
CAN

Proof All Things Work Together
For Your Good

HOLY
BIBLE

Tameka R. Bullock

ISBN: 978-1-945377-04-4
First Edition Printing
Printed in the United States of America
December 2017

Introduction

Hello, All! I am Evangelist Tameka R. Bullock the oldest sister of six born and raised in northern Philadelphia. I have two children who mean the world to me. I see myself as a caring, trusting, and very energetic person who loves to serve the Lord!

I am so excited for what God is doing in my life; I never thought that just being a church-going believer would save my life. As I grew in the Spirit, I then developed an intimate relationship that showed me how much I mean to God. God wants to use me for building His kingdom, and I want to be used by Him.

Although the story of my life hasn't been perfect, I praise God for saving me because that's what has gotten me through some dark times. Jeremiah 29:11 (NIV) *"For I know the plans I have for you, declares the Lord, plans to prosper you and not to harm you, plans to give you hope and future."*

I dedicate this book to the glory of God and in memory of my grandmother Lila McClure.

Chapter 1
Everything Has a Beginning

"Why me God?" was the question that I found myself asking daily during my early years. The oldest of six children, I was constantly left in charge of my siblings. My mother, who was using the drug called crack, stayed in bed daily with her man named, "Jack." Her thoughts were all over the place as she told us outrageous stories. She often would leave us home alone and come back and blame me for all of her daily woes.

I was beaten, burned, and scorned. Can you imagine all the pain I was forced to endure at only twelve years old? The pain was exhausting. The person who should have been giving me love was the same one causing me pain. At the age of twelve, I was responsible for the care of my siblings. Each day there was a constant reminder that drugs and alcohol would be present. All of this stemmed from the choices and decisions from the one who gave us life.

Sometimes I wondered why God chose me to be first born. Do I stay strong or do I cry? Is all of this my fault? I felt so lost and alone yet I had to remain positive for my siblings who looked to me for guidance. Often, I would wonder if my birth triggered some pain and hurt within her. This question continually haunts me. To this day I still do not have an answer. I always assumed our presence was the root of her animosity towards my siblings and I. Had our births stolen our mother's freedom too soon? Did she feel like she had more life to live before starting her family?

For the first decade of my life, it felt like I was standing in quicksand. Throughout my younger years, there was no structure; we moved from place to place and school to school. Finally, the day came when my mother was able to rent a huge house. She was incredibly excited, and for once I was very happy for her. The happiness was due to our family no longer being put out of other people's homes. I finally had my very own room. It felt like we were finally moving in the right direction, but the joy of having my room didn't last long.

My mother now became the host for the parties that lasted days at a time. "Why me God?" I belted out as the things around me continued to spin out of control. Alone in my room, I sat waiting for a response, but still, I heard nothing.

The neglect and abandonment grew stronger as the pain and weight of the life I was forced to live grew heavier. Being thrust into the role of mother for my sisters caused me to be labeled the mean, bossy, and controlling sister. All I ever wanted to do was shield them from the craziness that was now a part of our everyday lives. The reality was I needed them to be safe from the company that entered our home dressed as wolves dressed in sheep clothes)

Our family had already experienced a tragedy that made the news. These deaths left us in shock. We had to say goodbye to two of our family members at such an early age. I never knew the pain and feelings of helplessness of death until then. My family members had been murdered by a man who married into our family. I thought this could only happen on television. I was left feeling devastated after learning what happened. Due to this, I feared men and I could never get comfortable when they entered our home. Whether family, guest or a friend.

Our mother did not play when it came to wandering eyes towards my sisters and I. If a man looked at us too long or perversely she would check him real quick. Only our mother could treat us wrong. I believe she thought she was a great mom in that regard.

One night a big fight broke out that had involved my mother. She and her boyfriend had an altercation which caused her to fight for her life. I feared she wouldn't make it out of this detrimental relationship. My mother for some reason would always ended up in unhealthy circumstances with men and so called "friends" who had negative agendas from the start. Their focus was to get her high and then take advantage of her.

One good thing about my mother is that she has a very forgiving spirit. She would give her last just to please friends. Her kindness had led people to take advantage of her. As a result of being high, she neglected a lot of her motherly responsibilities. There were too many all-night parties. We had to stay in our bedrooms during these parties. We couldn't even get a good night sleep due to the loudness in the house. Sometimes we barely had food to eat for dinner. This was not enough to stop the parties. They would continue till dawn. My siblings and I lost sleep because we were afraid and did not know what would happen next during the parties.

My mind would constantly race through the night because we never knew what craziness lied ahead of us. So, we stayed ready to help my mother fight off the unwanted company just in case. *I always had her back no matter what family always came first.* Mother taught us well when it came to family. She would often tell us that blood is thicker than water and never forget to have each other's back.

These battles with her "friends" were becoming a part of our daily lives. It seemed strange when there was a calm night. When you're immune to violence and dysfunctional behaviors it eventually becomes your way of life. We waited for more drama as each night approached. We wondered what the evening would bring to our home.

My mother at times did show true love. She would buy juice & pizza. We would go food shopping at the first of each month, but the call of the drugs and alcohol wouldn't leave her side.

So here I am questioning God again, but still, there was no response. Low self-esteem moved in and invaded my emotions. I was ashamed and walked around embarrassed making up excuses for my mother, always telling lies so I can fit in. Meanwhile, my friends on the block had mothers, fathers with jobs, cars and lived in peaceful homes as far as I could see. They wore the latest style clothes to school. Daily they were dressed to impress. I, on the other hand, had to count on my grandmother to buy my clothes, shoes, coats and give me spending money. Once the newness wore off, I didn't want to go back to school because I knew the teasing would start over again.

Before I even reached my teenage years my spirit was dead. The life I was living had affected me in all sorts of ways. I became aggressive and angry most of the time. I wished with all that I had that I had a father to come to my rescue. My friend who was as close as a sister had the best dad in the whole universe. He taught us about real love. When I would come to visit he made sure I had my favorite drink Apple Cider. As a child, it would always make me feel special and loved. Every cup of apple cider represented love. Each cup help to lessen the pain of thinking about my home life. Still, I would question God," where are you, father?" But again no response, "why are you not here for me?" Eventually, I accepted the fact that I didn't have a father to show me, love. No one ever could tell me anything about my biological father. I felt as if I had sinned by asking. "who and where is my father?", "How come I have never met him?"

So many challenges have taken place in my young childhood. At the age of two, I was struck by a car while playing in the sprinklers outside. The age of 6 I was hit by a police officer while riding on the back of a bike. This incident left me in a coma. I often thought that I lived in a nightmare. All I wanted was to wake up from this horrific dream. It always felt like wishful thinking "Dear God where are you?" But still, there was no response.

If you look in my eyes, you'll see that survival lives there. The hurt I was forced to endure convinced me that this was what life was all about. One fall day my mother was hungover, and she slept till the next day, only to wake up to find out her party friends robbed the house. They helped themselves to food, toiletries and whatever else they wanted. I tried to tell them kindly to put our things down, but they yelled in my face and said that I was too grown and disrespectful. "You better stay in a child's place you're not grown". They yelled at me as I was threatening to call the cops. I angrily slammed the phone down. I was furious that they had called my bluff, so I called my grandmother instead. I tried to verbally defend my mother, but demonic curses were spoken over my life instead.

I was a 12-year-old girl who could see demonic spirits in action. Demons do not want to be seen, and they do not want to be told to leave. These spirits did not like that I was calling them out so instead they cursed me out and slammed the door in my face. The proper thing should have been for my mother to confront her frustrations on the friends who stole from her. However, she chose to work out her frustrations in other ways, me.

I decided on this day that she had to find another outlet for her anger. So when my mom went into an uncontrollable rage, I finally stood up for myself. I don't know what came over me, but dear God where are you? Surprisingly, my mother stopped in her tracks and called my grandmother. She yelled through the phone, "Come get her before I make her disappear from the face of the earth!" My grandmother arrived quickly to the scene. She gathered my belongings and escorted me into my New Beginning! She told my mother to get her life in order, or there will be grave consequences.

My grandmother had always demonstrated her love for me. She healed my physical, emotional, and spiritual wounds with the words from the Holy Bible. She promised that I would live and not die, she made sure I knew that I would make it through this difficult time. I cried as she held me tight that night. I had also asked my grandmother to please make sure that my sisters were alright. She replied, "The blood that Jesus shed is for them too." God has a purpose and plan outlined for you. What the Lord has created for good the enemy tries to taint for his evil desires. The Lord will always restore all that you have lost. He will give you a more abundant life greater than what you could ever dream. I did not know what in the world my grandmother meant by those words, but what I did know was that I was safe and loved. Living with her was such a tremendous blessing. I finished middle and high school with my head held high. I began to embrace who I was becoming. My self-esteem and self-worth began to rise. Finally, there were no more restless and sleepless nights, that season of my life had come to an end.

Life was beautiful until my senior year. Graduation night I decided to sneak out with my high school sweetheart. Sixty days later I found out that I was pregnant. All I could think about was my grandmother's words. My pregnancy could not have been part of the plans when she spoke into my life. She had rescued me from so much, and this is how I repaid her. I knew in my heart of hearts that I had let her down.

Just having my grandmother being furious with me was punishment enough. I finally worked up the courage to tell her that I was expecting a baby. Her response, "Tell me something that I don't know." Her response was both shocking and relieving all at the same time. In my mind, I thought, "WOW, she's not that upset." I thought that I was going to be ok. Her next breath carried an ultimatum that I wasn't ready to hear. "You have one week to abort and time is running out," she said. Let's get this distraction taken care of, and you will be all right." God has plans for you my grandmother would always say. However, she never told me the contents of His plans. I wanted to say to her that I am tired of hearing you repeat that to me over and over again. I'm wondering does God have plans for me or are they your plans? I kept my mouth shut and I took the information she handed me and replied: "If you think that's for the best."

For the next week, I just couldn't see myself terminating this pregnancy. There was a lot of was pressure to make a decision. Do I follow my grandmother's instructions to abort? Or do I become a mother? I told my High School sweetheart what she had suggested that I do, and he was livid. He went off about how could a so-called "Church lady" tell you to do something like that? God would never tell you to get rid of his creation he yelled. He promised me that he would never abandon his responsibilities and that he would always be there for our child. I trusted him and his words. I had hoped that we could be a happy family.

We later sat back to reminisce back on how we first fell in love. The year was 1986, and I had just made my grand entrance into the school gymnasium. Every year there was a Thanksgiving "Can Can" Dance held at my school. I knew I was fly that night. I wore my gold hand bone chain, big bamboo earrings, Lee's jeans with my favorite red and white Coca-Cola shirt. I walked out to the dance floor as the DJ was playing Eric B is President by Eric B. and Rakim. All of my classmates were on the floor getting into their groove and dancing.

Suddenly I looked up, and the love of my life stared at me right in the face. My mouth dropped as this handsome young man asked for a dance. On the inside, I was overwhelmed beyond belief. I tried to hold back my emotions, but my mouth gave me away. My friends and I were talking about the most popular boy in the whole school with the LL Cool J lips. I could not believe he wanted to dance with me. I responded with a big smile let's do this as we danced the night away. As we danced, I hoped the DJ would play for a lifetime.

As we fell out of our memories of the past, we both knew that our high school love story didn't mean anything to my grandmother. For just a quick moment it brought joy and peace to the decision we had to make.

The next evening I started planning our future together. I sat my grandmother down to talk. I explained to her that this is my life and I chose to start a new life with my boyfriend and our child.

Initially, my grandmother was enraged. Then after a few moments, she calmed down and said "You're right, but it won't happen under my roof. I expect you to be moved out by the end of my work day today." I never thought it would come to this. I had damaged our relationship and broke her trust in me. I picked up the phone and called my high school sweetheart and told him I had to leave home. I told him how I am no longer welcomed at my home as long as I keep the baby.

He apologized to me for the trouble I was in with my grandmother. I told him that what's done is done so we can't blame one another. I started to cry, and I asked him what's going to happen now? He had placed his grandmother on the phone to speak to me. She offered me a room. She knew I was pregnant and promised that we were in good hands. At first, I accepted the offer. However, for some reason, I didn't feel too comfortable with the decision I had just made.

So, later on, I went to my Angel's house, and I explained everything to her. My Angel was a sweet neighbor who lived on my mother's block. She had a gentle heart. She was the one person who always had my best interest in mind. I turned to her for counsel on this matter. I had no idea what to do next. I was not prepared for my family to write me off. I had not followed their plans for my life, and because of this, I had to leave home.

My Angel said that I should give my grandmother some time. She also believed that my grandmother would have a change of heart towards me. My Angel always took the time to mentor and redirected me despite my current situation. Even after I moved in with my grandmother, she kept in touch with me and treated me like I was her daughter. My Angel saw what was inside of me. She was willing to take the time to nurture what was there. Ever since we met me, she never left my side.

A few weeks after I left her house my grandmother came to look for me. She wanted to apologize for the way she handled everything. I accepted her apology, but I continued to stay with Angel until I got on my feet. I had gone to church with Angel one Sunday morning. I finally, let go of the guilt and hurt, and I made my way to the altar. I was pregnant and having a baby out of wedlock. I realized that I needed to accept the Lord Jesus as my savior.

Three years later I was a bride walking down the aisle! Our marriage was beautiful, and it was all that mattered to me. I had my very own world in which my husband and my child was my center. The enemy had used my deepest desires to pull me away from God. I had abandoned God and made the family that I had created into my god. I was caught up in my perfect self that I didn't give God any attention. I thought being a devoted wife was all it took to keep our marriage intact. I had never witnessed or had any examples of a good marriage. I relied on my intuitions since they had not failed me as yet. In my eyes, I was holding it down, and I was taking care of my husband's needs. I thought that keeping our home in order and being a loving mother was all that was required of me. This kind of mindset caused me to close the door on God and invited the enemy in instead.

My focus had been distorted so much that I didn't even see when my husband had become sucked into a life of infidelity. By the time I realized what was going on it was too late. He was deeply consumed in adultery while trying to maintain two families. I found myself in a place of unforgiveness, rage, and disappointment. I was back in survival mode all over again. However, this time I was sparking the fire by cursing him, stalking them, and trying to reclaim what was mine at the time. After a while, I got tired of arguing and fighting. All I wanted and needed was for the pain to end.

Dear God it's either going to be him or me. From this point on my heart was full of hatred towards my husband. I had grown closer to darkness. There was no light to force the darkness out of my heart. For a while the enemy had me bent out of shape. My life was filled with as much darkness as my heart. I never even turned a light on in my house. I wanted to be swallowed up by the darkness. I was mentally and physically drained. The betrayal was real in my eyes and my heart. God this was not how I planned my life.

Early one morning there was a loud knocking on my front door followed by a soft stern voice "Are you there? Open the door" I tried to hide the hurt before I let my grandmother in but the tears begin to roll down my cheeks as she embraced me. "You lost focus on the one who loves you the most. Give your life back to God for He's the only one who can take away your pain. Man will lie, sneak, cheat, steal your soul and lead you down the way that is broad and wide." Her words started to fill me up with light as she started to open the windows of my house. "Come out of the darkness your son still needs you to live."

Meanwhile, my husband chose to stay in his sin. The enemy convinced him that everything was just fine. He swore that he was cleared from all of his infidelities. He believed there was no reason for concern or alarm. Sin had convinced him that leaving his spouse and baby back at home to engage in illicit activity with someone who he had no business laying down with was ok. He was ok trying to delete his history to fit the story that he created for his other life. He was hoping I'd stay even though he gave our commitment away.

This is what the enemy wanted the whole time. He desired to destroy our family. I did not know how to win. I was gradually healing from the divorce and moved forward. I would walk around like I was ok but I was covering up the hurt with a fake smile. I was now out in the world living freely.

I found new and unhealthy experiences with the wrong people. I kept falling into the enemy's trap, and I let my flesh rule me. Nightclubs, after-hour parties, drinking and getting caught up in fornication, lust, and lies became my normal life. I would play church on Sundays. I prayed to God when I arrived, yet still, I was not accountable to Jesus Christ.

I was introduced to a counterfeit love by the one who promised me the moon and the stars above. One year later my baby girl enters the world. I am now a single mother. I hated feeling like the devil had played me. Am I running the same race my mom had started? Dear God, when will it ever end? The contrary voices had begun to invade my thoughts like a sickness that has settled within me. The voices are urging me to tie the noose around my throat, whispering that no one cares for me anymore.

When one day I looked at the "Raine" I had remembered the morning. I loved the feeling of clean, fresh linen against my skin as I woke up. I anticipated the arrival of my baby girl. I reminded myself not to worry or fear.

The time of delivery had arrived, and I couldn't be more scared. My child has decided that she is ready to take on the world. I, on the other hand, was not close to being ready.

The contractions began, and I needed my sister to take me to the hospital. "Sister are we almost there?" I scream as I am having painful contractions in the back seat. As we arrive at the emergency room, I was covered in sweat and tears. Twenty-two hours later there was a newcomer in the hospital room. My daughter had finally made her grand entrance it into the world. I no longer saw life as this dark black and white place. When I looked at my daughter, I saw beautiful color.

It still amazes me how much the Lord has blessed me. Yes, Lord, this is the day that you have made, and I shall rejoice and be glad in it! Once the nurse laid her on my chest, I felt the "Raine" flood my life. The nine months of feeling ashamed were being washed out. It felt like I received a renewed vigor for life. God had allowed a beautiful shower to bring forth new growth in my life. I dropped to my knees, told the demons that tormented me to leave me alone. "Father God please forgive me for worshipping man instead of you. Forgive me for all my sins. Father God, I terminate my partnership with the enemy's camp. I fully submit my life to you in the Name of Jesus." I prayed that prayer with a sincere heart. I genuinely wanted God to do a new thing in my life.

I looked around, and God had shifted my whole atmosphere. The people, places, and things that I had indulged in God had replaced with a heart of worship. I was learning how to fast and pray for real with saved sisters in Christ. The stronger I grew in God, the angrier the devil became. The devil was always trying to come up with all kinds of ways to bring me back to his kingdom.

Once the devil saw that attacking me wasn't working, he decided to go after those closest to me. The devil came after my son. He tried to take him from this world. I had just left a revival. While there, I was led to intercede on behalf of my son. I prayed for him to be safe from the neighborhood gangs.

Hours later the police tracked me down to deliver some bad news. "Ma'am your son took a bullet to his head, and it doesn't look like he'll be around much longer." I grabbed my keys, and I prayed to God. I asked not to allow early death to be his destiny. *God, please have mercy on my son's life.* God's peace and comfort suddenly wrapped around like a warm blanket and I knew deep in my heart that my son would not die.

The doctors said that it's a chance that he will never be the same. Two months later God changed their report and they thought it that it was luck, but I knew it was his mother's prayers.

I thought I could plan my own life out down to the last detail. However, God had already ordained a purpose and a plan for my life. God being the patient God that He is just waiting for me to come into agreement with His plan. The Bible says in Romans 8:28 *"And we know that in all things God works for the good of those who love him, who has been call according to his purpose."*

I pray that you will accept Jesus Christ into your life. The minute that you are born you receive a call on your life to build up God's kingdom and to walk according to His purpose. No matter what the enemy puts in your way you are to grow through the situation. Don't give up and always keep God first. Trust and believe He will work it out for your good. God did it for me, and God will do it for you. I pray that you will live and not die in Jesus Name Amen!

Chapter 2
Seemed Like God Was Always In My Business

It has always been my heart desire to be a blessing to the unfortunate. The way my childhood started out, I would never wish that on anyone. I know that a child should never have to go through what I experienced.

Back in 1991, a sibling was born four months early due to drug and alcohol poisoning. She was hospitalized for months. My sibling needed special home care that we were not able to provide. No one in the family was able to care for her properly. My sibling had to be given over to a foster home as a result. This situation disturbed me, but it was out of my control. We were allowed to visit her and stay in close contact. The foster family gave her excellent care. They were very kind in communicating with our family about my sibling's progress. They raised her like their very own so much so that they adopted her later. From that point on I knew that I would return the same blessing to other children.

Now I'm a mentor and foster parent willing to go the extra mile to see a child's frown turn upside down. Who better to identify with the hurt and the struggles that these kids are going through than someone who's already been through it? I've been there and made it out alive. I believe, God had already set me up for a time such as this. I couldn't understand it when I was going through, but I was growing through my past hurts.

I remember my first job at the age of 14 working at a daycare inside the Salvation Army. I helped kids learn how to read and write, and it was a great experience. I enjoyed it so much that every summer I applied there for a job. I just felt the need to return the favor, give back to the community and make my own money all at the same time.

God was setting me up in more ways than one. He was allowed me to give the love that I never received. I loved those kids the way that I wished that I had been loved. Young people are dear to my heart. I had worked in a retail business and youth would gravitate towards me. They trusted and valued my opinion. I sometimes wondered what my life would be like if I had never experienced a dysfunctional family.

In every step of the way, I found God to be in my business. He had held me in His hands when I thought that I was the devil's property. I believed I was a cursed. I had been consumed by doubt, frustration, and broken promises for 20 years. I couldn't see the blessing in the midst of it all. God was in my business when I needed it the most. He sent me wise counsel who taught me how to reclaim what I had lost. They helped me to rename what God had already provided for me.

I thank God for Apostle Owen Ford Jr. because God used him mightily to show me the blessings I received. I am learning that God's timing is not my timing. I have also discovered that God is always on time. God was starting me out with a good foundation. It was the devil's job to keep me from seeing my potential and His blessing. Yes, God does have a plan for your life. I am a living witness. The Bible says in 2 Timothy 1:9 *"For God saved us and called us to live a holy life."* He did this not because we deserved it but because that was His plan from before the beginning of time to show us His grace through Jesus Christ. The word of God helps me understand why I was created.

God has saved you. He has called you as His own. This means if you are born again you are on your first step to answering God's call for your life. It may seem difficult to understand, but Jesus saved you and called you according to His purpose and grace. Are you finding that you are in an awkward place? Please know that you are not forgotten. God is concerned about you. God has to take you through some things to prepare you for the next stage in your life. He desires for you to operate in excellence. The things that you're going through will be a blessing to the next person who life depends on your testimony.

Believe that God has a purpose in life for you to fulfill. You are not a coincidence. You must always remember that your life matters. The Bible says in 2 Timothy 5:10 *"For we must all appear before the all-night seat of Christ; that every one may receive the things done in his body, according to that he hath done, whether it be good or bad."* So, no matter what state you find yourself in remember that you are there to produce for the kingdom of God. Your goal should be to bring the lost into the saving knowledge of Jesus Christ.

God has always been in your business. He has had your back since before you ever came out of your mother's womb. On the day of judgment, you will give an account for what you've done with your purpose and calling. I pray that as you're reading this right now, you will come into agreement that God has saved you. He has called you to live a holy life. If you call on the name of Jesus, ask for forgiveness, Then open your heart. Let the Lord of, host in so He can reveal His plan for you.

If you are not saved and born again, I pray that the word of God will encourage you. Repent and accept Jesus Christ into your life right now in Jesus name I pray amen.

Chapter 3
I Did It My Way

There was a time I felt like the children of Israel out in the wilderness walking in circles for forty years with no purpose. They blamed their failures on God. Then as time passed they eventually died. I too found myself placing blame on people, situations, and most of all God for my very own self-destruction. I could have lost my life due to my disobedience. However, God saw fit to love me in spite of my flaws and shortcomings. I accepted the Lord Jesus Christ as my personal savior at the age of 18, with my first child growing in my womb. I was confident and sure that God had forgiven me, especially, since I became pregnant outside of marriage. I was on fire for God. Prayer and praise were all I preferred to do. I couldn't get enough fellowship with the people of God. I loved to be in his presence. My blessings were flowing left and right. God had allowed my child to be born healthy. I became a wife, had a wonderful home. I even had a great job. God had done more than enough for me, and I was excited to share the good news. My life now is grand. I'm able to do whatever I want to. I had the car, the money, the best clothes, and my plans were finally working out.

As the days went on, I started depending on myself and slowly distancing myself from God. Prayer and praise became scarce. Fasting seemed like a thing of past. My Sunday fellowships became lighter and lighter. The time came where I ultimately left the church. I found myself caught up in self-pity. I indulged in adultery, fornication and harbored feelings of bitterness. Envy and unforgiveness showed up due to my rebellion. God had an ordained time for the children of Israel to go into the promised land. God had taken them out of Egypt. However, they still missed their purpose in life due to their doubt and unbelief. I found myself feeling like I lost my goal. I asked myself whether it mattered if I lived or died. I often wondered if it mattered if I was hurting? Why did it matter if I'm trying my best to achieve what God had for me if my best isn't good enough? It felt like it didn't matter if I did right or wrong. The hurt and pain that I felt were unbearable. I was living with it. I had taken up residence on unbelief boulevard. It was a sweet home. As I became comfortable in this new house, I would ask myself questions. Does it matter if I run to God or run away? Should I pray for help? Or allow myself to be preyed upon? Does it matter if I'm drunk or sober? How about being gay or straight? Does it matter if I accept God or deny Him?

The answer lies in John 3:16 "God so loved the world that he gave his only begotten son that whoever shall believe in him shall not perish but have everlasting life." God had already shown himself to be true in my life. He delivered his promises. I, however, forgot all that he had done in my life just that quick. Not only was I committing adultery while I was in the world. I was also committing spiritual adultery. The bible says in James 4:4 "Adulterers and adulteresses!

Do you not know that friendship with the world is enmity with God? Whoever therefore wants to be a friend of the world makes himself an enemy of God." The Bible tells us that people who choose to be friends with the world are an adulterous people. I had become that person who was so happy and content with the marriage, child, cars, money, friends, the clubs and other people's business that I had made them my god.

The moment I let my life be my god that's when all hell broke loose. I was fighting in the war. However, I wasn't dressed for the battle. I had nothing to protect me. I had no belt of truth nor a breastplate of righteousness. I did not have peace in my life or a shield of faith. I also did not have a helmet of salvation to protect me. My sword to fight the devil was too heavy for me to lift. I did not have any power to raise it. God has allowed me to lose some things. I had to go through life-changing situations just for him to get me to refocus. I am forever grateful that I didn't lose my life over my disobedience.

The Bible says that God is married backslider but are you committed to your marriage with God? Don't get divorced by God for not being committed to Him. You can't have it both ways it's either the world or heaven. The Bible says in Revelations 3:15-16 "I know your deeds, that you are neither cold nor hot. I wish you were either one or the other so because you are lukewarm neither hot nor cold I'm about to spit you out of my mouth." Listen you don't want this to happen to you because your divorce could be final. I encourage you to save your marriage to God.

Israel became like an adulterous wife who wanted both a husband and another lover. In the Bible Hosea 6:1 NKJV "Come and let us return unto the Lord; For He has torn, but He will heal us; he has stricken, but He will bind us up."

I pray in the name of Jesus that if you're in need of a divorce from worldly things that you separate from the devil. I pray that you will serve the enemy his divorce papers immediately in the name of Jesus. You shall no longer be connected to the spirits of fornication, homosexuality, envy, depression, and disease. I bind all the forms of idolatry that would try to disguise itself and attach onto you as a friendly relationship. In the name of Jesus, it will not work, and it will have no dominion over you or your marriage with

Jesus Christ. Your yes to your vowel renewal to Jesus Christ will now produce the good fruits of the spirit. Galatians 5:22-23 (NIV) "But the fruit of the spirit is love, joy, peace, forbearance, kindness, goodness, faithfulness, gentleness, and self-control. Against such things, there is no law." I pray that you will be successful and that you will gain eternal life in the name of Jesus I pray, Amen!

Chapter 4

The F. O. G. Is More Than Enough (Favor Of God)

It took some time for me to understand that the favor of God was all I ever needed in my life. I planned to survive by any means necessary. This mindset caused me to stay in unhealthy relationships.

I was worried about how my bills would get paid with the salary that I brought home. I always wanted to be able to wine and dine with my friends, book flights, and spend nights in luxury hotels. I yearned for what I considered the good life. I did not believe my salary would allow this good life to be achieved on my salary.

I decided to deal with deception and disappearing acts. I convinced myself that these type of relationships would benefit me soon. I surrendered to the lies. While I knew deep down inside that, he wasn't the right man for me. We were unevenly yoked. We shouldn't have been together, but our fornication kept us intertwined.

I planned and organized dates to spend time together as a couple. However, the counterfeit love that we had finally showed its true face. All my plans went to waste. I thank God for His grace and mercy that saved me from my selfish plans.

God's never-ending love has freed me from the sins that held me captive for so long. I believed that God could fix me and restore the time that I had lost. I surrendered myself to Jesus Christ, and now I am the new TAMEKA to God be the Glory!

T- Turning my life to Jesus

A- Arriving by God's grace and favor

M- Making the transformation

E- Eternal life

K- Keeping God first

A- acknowledging I am a sinner

If you're reading this and you have not yet accepted God as your personal savior, I want you to pray this prayer with me.

"God, thank you for coming into my life. Forgive me for all the times I closed you out of my life, and the times I chose to only consider me and not you. I repent with all my heart. I surrender my whole life to you in the Name of Jesus Amen!"

The Favor of God allowed me to change the meaning of my name to represent who I am in Christ today! Grace accepts the new Tameka. I am no longer held hostage by the old me or what anyone in this world thinks of me. The Bible says in 2 Corinthians 5:17 (NIV) *"Therefore, if anyone is in Christ, the new creation has come. The old has gone, the new is here!"*

HALLELUJAH, I am walking in the new life that God has given me, and it feels stupendous. People tend to believe that money, power, and respect is the key to life but that's a lie from the pit of hell. The enemy wants you to believe that without having status or notoriety you're at the bottom of the barrel like a crab fighting to stay alive. But not so I am a witness all you need is C.R.E.A.M. (Christ. Rules. Everything. Around. Me). Once you take on a Christ-like mindset, you are an overcomer!

No, I don't have the six-figure job, but I do have a job. This job allows my daughter and I to live comfortably. God has favored us.

> *God is more than enough, open the can of God's plan for your life and live on purpose.*

The new Tameka is called to Evangelize. She will spread the good news by any means necessary. I pray for the person reading this right now that you will have an abundance of faith that will make you whole. Whatever you are in need of God will give you favor beyond what you can ever imagine. You'll never be caught up in sinful arrangements ever again. The favor of God is all you will ever need in Jesus Name I pray, Amen!

Chapter 5

Just Some Inspirational Notes

You have the authority to command your day. You must have faith in what you speak. Declare life over yourself, and all that concerns you, and it shall come to pass.

P. L. A. L. (Praise, Laugh, and Live)
Never forget to praise, laugh, and live. Praise God for all of the great and wonderful things for you. Take a moment to think about how God has blessed you. Some great and mighty things have occurred in your life. There is more to you than just waking up in the morning.

God has blessed you and covered you all throughout your life. He has protected you from death. The devil desires to sift you as wheat. However, God has said not so. He has declared that you shall live a prosperous and healthy life.

We all have made some questionable decisions in life. God should have punished us. Instead, He saw fit to forgive us. Instead, He has extended us mercy. So, shout out your love for God from the rooftops. The Lord deserves all of the glory and honor. If we want the blessings that God has for us to rain down, we must send the praises up to God.

There is a saying that laughter is the best medicine. Laughter will make you feel a little lighter. Anxiety, depression, and other such demonic spirits will leave with a little laugh.

Life can be stressful, and it can take a toll on our lives. Tense situations, anger, and feelings of helplessness will cause you to make wrong decisions. The devil's goal is to make you act out of character. One of the best ways to make him mad is by laughing in his face. You can declare that he has no power in your life.

Most importantly you need to live. You need to live your life and enjoy all of God's splendor. God wants us to have a prosperous life. He desires for you to live according to his purpose. This doesn't mean that we have to be bored at home in a corner. There are amazing and fun places to go. You can have good wholesome fun. You no longer have to play in the world's playground. There are many things in this world for us to enjoy. Go out and enjoy all God has created.

Command your day from the moment you wake up. Pray to our Father in heaven. Make sure you tell Him all of your heart's desires. Praise, Laugh and Live all the way through the problem as the devil tries to distract you. Knock him in the head because he has no power in your life. Praise the fact God has got your back. Laugh out loud because you are still intact. Live so that you can unlock the truth that Jesus Christ is waiting for you to receive.

Poems From the Heart

The next part of this book is just a few poems that God gave me to share with you. I pray that these words continue to touch your heart and make it pliable to what God has to say to you.

The Gift

Money and diamonds rule this world
Man is twisted by getting turned up on negative energy
Making excuses for their future, sleeping with sorrow like there's no tomorrow
Being misled so they can stay in bed covered up in filthy threads
Don't you know the devil wants your head?
Read all about it God's not dead
John 14:6 (NIV) says "I am the way and the truth and the life. No one comes to the father except through me."
God's love is a gift that I've never had before, and you give me strength to soar for more
My eyes are open like the red sea
Eternal life with God is the only thing that can satisfy me!

Tameka R. Bullock [53]

The Storm

The storm is near but there's no need to fear look around, God will guide you through

My God, My God He is here to stay

My spirit is filled with Him, the wave of salvation is here for me to ride

The winds are blowing, and the angels are singing

Sweet sounds fill the land, beautiful white sand sparkles through the tide

Hear me clear, let me reign and my love will take away all the pain

I gave man breath; now he can stand and witness the splendors of life

Jesus took on the ultimate sacrifice

His death covers you and makes you a survivor

The storms of life will rage, but you are covered under the almighty shelter

Genesis 2:7 (NIV) "Then the Lord God formed a man from the dust of the ground and breathed into his nostrils the breath of life, and the man became a living being."

Faith, Love, and Hope

Beloved, Beloved I stretched my hands to you, so proud you grabbed onto
No more neglect, the abandonment is gone
He now lives in you so close your mouth open your heart
Let HIs glory tell your story, Jesus left the way for you
God wants you to adapt to him this season
Victory was won the day Jesus hung on the cross
Your old background was destroyed, and the devil's clearances are null and void
You are a new creature ready for war
Put on the whole Armor of God

Ephesians 6:10 (NIV) *"Finally, be strong in the Lord and in his mighty power."*

The Promise

God Covenant is evident as it appears way up in the clouds
Red, orange, and consuming fire beams of yellow blazing so bold and bright
Green and blue reflections of loyalty looking straight at you
Purple and white shows the world its pure power all through the Earth
The rainbow sits high above just to remind us of God's love!

Genesis 9:13 (NIV) *"I have set my rainbow in the clouds, and it will be the sign of the covenant between me and the earth."*

Forgiveness

If you knew what you were born to do, would you blink
your eyes lay down and die
Not realizing why God created you to Survive
The blood Jesus has shed without any doubt
He brought your sins spreading on the cross bruised
in all
Cleanse your hearts and sustain purity in this life and
you will become royalty
Wipe out the deceit, take off the disguise and let the
True Love of Christ consume your past resentment
Punishment is no longer an option so forgive yourself
go on letting victory rule and win don't get stuck in sin
again

Matthews 6:14-15 (NIV) *"For if you forgive other people
when they sin against you,
Your heavenly father will also forgive you, but if you do
not forgive others their sins your father will not forgive
your sins"*

Tameka R. Bullock [57]

Don't Be Left Behind

Body on life support mind traveling through different dimensions

Feelings of guilt since you never honored God wishing this was a dream screaming at the demons

You thought that you were doing well while on earth, you thought that winning souls was all that you had to do

Oh how wrong you were and all the while your soul was in shambles

Thrown into the burning furnace to live forever in a hell hole

I lost track of the time

I couldn't even repent or trade my sins in

Today is my date

And time got away

I guess that I missed the holy gates

Romans 6:23 (NIV) *"For the wages of sin is death, but the gift of God is eternal life in Christ Jesus our Lord."*

Soul Ties

I thought he loved me I thought I was the one and the only one.

Guess what I thought wrong, man will lie, mislead and take advantage of you

My brethren seek the Lord first and ask God for guidance in all that you do

Going ahead of God will have you believing what Lucifer puts before you is the real deal

It looks good, feels great, and sounds so delightful that you indulge all night

You wake up like wow that was a great night

You have now entered Lucifer's camp, and your mind, body, and soul are being attacked

Lucifer's spirits now have you blind, deaf and lost you don't know what's going on your soul is under his control

You're in good hands I own you, my love

I will never do you wrong as long, as you stay with me your debts are paid

I will always keep you protected since I, Lucifer am your god

Lucifer has sure blinded you as time still moves while you're consuming lies, abandonment, frustration, and abuse what's the use

Tameka R. Bullock [59]

No one wants me now I have no juice
Peers are tweeting "kill yourself and die."
This is what Lucifer imparted inside
Beloved, he never loved you he took you on a ride down the dark side
Brethren, please break the ties run to Jesus his arms are open
He will never forsake you, mistreat you or tell you lies for he built you to survive
He gave up the ghost so you can have a choice now or eternity
Who will you host?

John 1-1:9(NIV) *"If we confess our sins, he is faithful and just and will forgive us our sins and purify us from all unrighteousness."*

Unlawful Airways

The Vines have invaded the land dropping demonic connection through the tubes that you choose to watch

You've fallen victim to the chat rooms that allow snakes to take a bite out of your Apple and destroy your galaxy

The demonic connection blocks the reality of God's vision

Pinterest now has your interest, and you always take a second look at Facebook

You tweet all day long and post to Instagram

Wi-Fi is the official lifeline

Don't get caught in the drop zone or your device will not receive the Good News

Follow the creator of everything for with him upgrades are free and two-year plans are canceled out

All warranties are extended to accept the terms and conditions for eternal life

Now that's a contract

Romans 10:9-10(NIV) "If you declare with your mouth, Jesus is Lord and believe in your heart that God raised him from the dead, you will be saved. For it is with your heart that you believe and is justified, and it is with your mouth that you profess your faith and are saved."

<hr>

Angel in Disguise

When trusting Bloodlines write you off, simply because you didn't follow the lines that were written for the script

Despite the fact that God called me for this role the director hollers cut you are not ready for this role

If you choose to take the lead, your career won't uphold

You have a week to terminate your contract then we can retake your lines you will be just fine

I tried to convince the director to see it's my choice, but the writer said clean out your dressing room and go

Now I'm carrying my story wondering how I will secure it

That's when my Angel came to the set

Psalm 91:11 (NIV) *for he will command his angels concerning you to guard you in all your ways*

<hr>

I Am Here

Sometimes I wondered why I was born first
Should I laugh or should I cry? Is it all my fault? Am I the one to blame?
No one is there for me through the flames
I'm lost and so alone my plate is very large, yet my sisters look at me like I am in charge
I feel the squeeze of the clouds
I yield, I yield I am over here God!
Do you see me I need a place to run to, did you say to follow you?
Yes, come to me, I was there even when you wondered who really cared
Your face has always been in my book you had just never taken a look
Now that I'm posted in your heart you see my status is love
I first so loved the world and you were born first through me
Love has always abounded in you-you're at a place where my spirit can grow free
True love church I thank God for you

Tameka R. Bullock [63]

John 3:16 (NIV) *"For God so loved the world that he gave his only begotten son, that who so ever believe in him should not perish but have eternal life."*

A Pastors Heart

This poem is dedicated to my pastors

Pastors are love chosen from above hearts are open like the church doors

All walks of life enter in and souls everything off of Jesus Christ words

Bondage, chains, heartaches are all broken, and lives are now shifted into new yokes

Apostle Owen and Julia Ford truly care about your spiritual welfare

They stand in the gap interceding on your behalf believing the promises God has made

Trusting the one who created the heavens and earth

True Love Pastor's submit their lives to Christ giving themselves away

So people don't go astray get lost or just simply run away

Hey, would you lose sleep answer calls in between your personal walls?

True love pastors are on assignment instructed from The Holy Kingdom

They have been charged and fully submitted to the call

People, please show your Pastors true love

1st Thessalonians 5:12-13 (NIV) *"Now we ask you, brothers and sisters, to acknowledge those who work hard among you, who care for you in the Lord and who admonish you. Hold them in the highest regard in love because of their work. Live in peace with each other."*

Are You Committed

Commitment is work within itself, but you accept the responsibility
You treat it like a 9 to 5 as if it owes you something in return
Waiting on your bi-weekly paycheck to hold over till the next
The next check is set to arrive as I'm still questioning how come I am still in a bind
When you are only loyal to the world and have no faith to commit to the journey, this is what manifests in your life
Anxiety, frustration, depression, and sin
Remember you only clocked in for 8 hours of time that's not enough to cover you through the end
So it's time to live and not die are you going to be committed or just dedicated to your shift?

Tameka R. Bullock [65]

Even Merriam Webster tells us to be committed means to put into charge or trust

Commit your life to God today your burdens will surely be shifted away

Paul followed the Lord's example of commitment and sacrifice and service

In Galatians 2:20 (NIV) *"I have been crucified with Christ, and I no longer live, but Christ lives in me. The life I now live in the body, I live by faith in the Son of God, who loved me and gave himself for me."*

Total devotion to God means to be committed to Jesus Christ!

I pray that these inspirational thoughts will be a blessing to you in some way shape or form. I pray that you are motivated every day to stay in communication with our heavenly father. I pray that you will open up God's plan and do all that he has planned for you. I pray that God will open your eyes to show you all the areas in your life that are not pleasing to him. I pray he gives you strength to remove any sin that will weigh you down and prevent your close relationship with him from prospering. I pray that you will increase your faith to the next level. I pray the person who hasn't accepted Jesus Christ as their personal savior will accept God and be born again in the name of Jesus. Join a true love Bible Teaching Church in Jesus name I pray Amen!

Special Thanks

To all of **my family and friends** thank you for all your love and support over the years. May God continually rain down blessings upon your life.

Gary and Tavia I love you two with all my heart. The two of you remind me of why I have to be obedient to what God called me to do. God has trusted me with your life. I'm so honored to have this opportunity to be called your Mother. I refused to be disobedient to God. I refuse to be a disappointment to you. I will strive to be the best example of my grandmother with lots of integrity. Proverbs 20:7 (NIV) *"The righteous lead blameless lives; blessed are their children after them."* #Teamwawg #WeAllWeGot

Minister Valerie McCaskill! I love you to life. Thanks for always being there in the midnight hours praying me through. Thanks for never turning your back on me. You make sure I see God in every situation of my life. Only God knew what I was anticipating doing that dreadful day. I know He sent you, my angel in disguise to tell me it's not worth it. You made sure I knew how much God loved me. From that moment on I knew you were a gift from God.

To **my Angel**, when everyone else shut their doors on me you opened your heart and showered me with love. You truly made me believe that angels exist. Without any hesitation, you loved my children and I. **Odaris A. Carter** I love you for life!

I'd like to send a final thank you out to my two brothers in Christ who helped me tremendously with my first book. My brother **Shelton Taylor** captured the pictures on the cover. Brother **Owen Ford III** did an amazing job editing the book. He helped me put my thoughts down onto paper. I'd like to shout out to the graphic design team at the **Artful Kingdom** for creating an amazing cover for my book.

I'm grateful to God for sending me to **True Love Church** where I'm under the leadership of **Apostles Owen and Julia Ford**. Apostles, I truly thank you for teaching me the importance of being planted, consisted, and rooted in the Word.

In the last four years, I have experienced all my spiritual first. This will always be with me. You demonstrated what true love looks like. You teach the word of God in love, flow in love, correct in love. Most of all you truly love our **Father** in heaven for real. You are great examples to the Kingdom. I am so blessed to be a daughter of **True Love Church**.

Take God's Plan Out of the Can [72]